The Aleph-Bais Trip on the Aleph-Bais Ship

Dedicated to my children, Mendel, Mushka, and Levi, with love. C.A.

Dedicated with love and gratitude to my daughters, Esther Avigail, Mayim Sarah, and Baila Pearl. B.B.

Lovingly dedicated to Moshe Holtzberg, may he live and be well, and to the blessed memory of his parents, Gavriel and Rivkah Holtzberg, Hy"d.

First Edition - 5769 / 2009
Fifth impression - Tevet 5777 / January 2017

Editor: D.L. Rosenfeld
Managing Editor: Yossi Leverton
Layout: Eli Chaikin

ISBN: 978-1-929628-25-4
LCCN: 2009900068

HACHAI PUBLISHING
Brooklyn, New York
Tel: 718-633-0100 Fax: 718-633-0103
www.hachai.com - info@hachai.com

Printed in China

בס"ד

The Aleph-Bais Trip
on the
Aleph-Bais Ship

by Chani Altein
illustrated by Baruch Becker

Hachai
PUBLISHING

Here's what happened one fine summer day:

ALEPH called, "**BAIS, VAIS, GIMMEL, DALET, HEY!**
Let's get together and take a trip,
A nice long ride on the Aleph-Bais Ship."

So **HEY** called **VOV**, who told **ZAYIN** and **CHES**,

"Come right away, and share the news with **TES**."

Flip, flap together, every single letter,
Each one is great, but together we are better!

YUD, KOF and CHOF brought FINAL CHOF with them,
Followed by LAMED, MEM and FINAL MEM.

NUN and FINAL NUN, SAMACH and AYIN,
PEY, FEY and FINAL FEY, all came flyin'.

Whoosh, swoosh together, every single letter,
Each one is great, but together we are better!

TZADDIK and **FINAL TZADDIK**, ready for fun,
Greeted **KOOF** and **RAISH**
As they came on the run.

Then **S**HIN and **S**IN, together with **T**OF,
Hurried to their friends,
Who'd waited long enough.

Splish, splash together, every single letter,
Each one is great, but together we are better!

Now where was **Sof**,
The last of the crew?

ALEPH, BAIS, VAIS
And GIMMEL had no clue!
DALET, HEY and VOV
Searched high and low,
ZAYIN, CHES and TES said,
"We don't know."

"Here's an idea," YUD told KOF and CHOF,

"Let's use our ship to look around for SOF."

FINAL CHOF, LAMED, MEM and FINAL MEM

Started to ask for help from Hashem.

With **N**UN, **F**INAL **N**UN, **S**AMACH, **A**YIN and **P**EY,

FEY and **F**INAL **F**EY checked every which way.

The letter **Tzaddik** peered, **Final Tzaddik** stared,
Koof, **Raish** and **Shin** stretched
as far as they dared.

Then **Sin** cried out, as loud as could be,
  "**Sof** is stuck in seaweed and trapped at sea!"

Tof cast the anchor, and while **Sof** held tight,
The letters pulled him in with all their might.
"Now we're together!" **Aleph** gave a shout,

"Letters, are you ready? Let's sail on out!"

Zip, zap together, every single letter,
Each one is great, but together we are better!

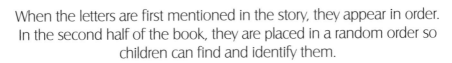

When the letters are first mentioned in the story, they appear in order.
In the second half of the book, they are placed in a random order so
children can find and identify them.

We have illustrated the Aleph-Bais using black characters on white
backgrounds. This will help children focus on the unique shape of
each letter, without the distraction of color. The letters Tzaddi and Final Tzaddi
are also called Tzaddik and Final Tzaddik (preface to the Zohar: Bereishis, 2b),
and we have chosen the latter pronunciation.

Note to Parents and Teachers:

Depending on your child's age, you may choose to focus on only one
letter per week or per day and reinforce its shape in some of the
following ways.

- Use clay, paint, or cookie dough to form the letter.
- Think of people whose names begin with that letter.
- Have your child point to a particular letter appearing numerous times
  on a page of a Siddur, Chumash, or other holy book.
- Cut out a letter and hide it around the room for your child to find.
- Make up a story that highlights the shape of each letter.
  Bais has a bench on the back; Mem has a peak like a mountain.
- Place a round object in the middle of the "dot letters."
  Give Bais a ball, Kof a candy, Pey a penny, and Tof, a cherry tomato!

Thanks to Draizy Zelcer for her creative ideas.

Glossary

Chumash . . . . One volume of the Five Books of Moses
Hashem . . . . G-d
Siddur . . . . Prayer Book